20 Answers

℘

Mormonism

Trent Horn

Catholic Answers Press

20 Answers: Mormonism

Trent Horn

© 2015 Catholic Answers

Published by Catholic Answers, Inc.

2020 Gillespie Way

El Cajon, California 92020

1-888-291-8000 orders

619-387-0042 fax

catholic.com

Printed in the United States of America

978-1-941663-23-3

978-1-941663-24-0 Kindle

978-1-941663-25-7 ePub

Introduction

Although many find Mormons to be caring and whole-some people, that alone is not a good reason to join their church. In fact, that isn't good a reason to join *any* church. A person should join a church because its teachings are true, because Jesus Christ founded it to guide believers to salvation. This short booklet will not examine every Mormon doctrine or practice to see if it's true, but rather the most important areas of disagreement between Mormonism and Catholicism. Are the Mormon teachings in those areas true or false?

I hope that Mormon readers will not think I am attacking their church. After all, Mormonism claims that the Catholic Church is not Christ's true Church. Mormons believe that *their* church is "the only true and living church upon the face of the whole earth."[1] I would not label a Mormon believer who made such a claim an "anti-Catholic." Instead, I would carefully listen to his arguments and see if he is right. I ask readers of this booklet, Mormon and non-Mormon alike, to extend me the same courtesy.

A note on terms: Because the Book of Mormon is their scripture, LDS are also commonly called Mormons, and so this booklet also uses that term. Additionally, although LDS call themselves a "church," from a Catholic perspective, strictly speaking, they are not. But for sake of simplicity, we will use the term here.

1. What is the Church of Jesus Christ of Latter-day Saints, and what makes it unique?

The Church of Jesus Christ of Latter-day Saints believes it has restored the doctrines of the early Church that were lost shortly after the death of the apostles. Latter-day Saints (or Mormons) believe that this restoration began in the year 1820, when 14-year-old Joseph Smith Jr. prayed for guidance about which Church he should join. Smith claimed that while he was praying in a grove of trees in upstate New York, two "personages" identifying themselves as God the Heavenly Father and Jesus Christ appeared to him. They allegedly told Smith that he was to join none of the currently existing churches. The LDS official website says:

> Over time, Joseph Smith was chosen to establish Christ's Church and restore the priesthood, or the authority to act in God's name. He was led by God to an ancient record and given the ability to translate it into English. This record is called the Book of Mormon. He continued to pray and receive revelation for the Church throughout his life. These revelations were compiled into a book of scriptures referred to as the Doctrine and Covenants and shows that God still leads His children today. Joseph Smith formally organized The Church of Jesus Christ of Latter-day Saints on April 6, 1830.[2]

As the Mormons spread throughout the Midwest, they came into conflict with other settlers who viewed their lifestyle and beliefs as a threat to the public well-being. Because of this conflict, most of the Mormons, including Smith, left Missouri and founded the town of Nauvoo, Illinois.

In 1844, several former leaders within the LDS church published a newspaper called *The Nauvoo Expositor* that accused Joseph Smith of introducing "false and damnable doctrines into the Church."[3] The Nauvoo city council, where Smith served as the town's mayor, declared the paper a nuisance and ordered its destruction.

In response to the destruction of the *Nauvoo Expositor's* printing press, the governor of Illinois ordered Joseph Smith to surrender himself to the authorities. Smith and his brother Hyrum were later arrested and held in the Carthage city jail on charges of treason. On June 27, 1844, an armed mob stormed the jail and engaged in a shootout with Smith while he was still in custody. Smith used a pistol that had been smuggled into the jail to fire several shots at his attackers before he was fatally wounded.[4]

Smith's close friend Brigham Young succeeded him as head of the church, and the entire church moved west to Salt Lake City, where its headquarters exists to this day.

It is estimated that, as of 2013, there were more than 15 million members of the Church of Jesus Christ of Latter-day Saints.[5]

Along with its fundamental doctrines about God, Christ, and salvation, Mormonism is different from Christian churches in the following ways:

- Christian churches believe that only the Bible is the inspired written word of God. But, according to their eighth article of faith, Mormons "believe the Bible to be the word of God as far as it is translated correctly; we also believe the Book of Mormon to be the word of God." Mormons believe that the works *Doctrine and Covenants* and the *Pearl of Great Price* are as inspired as the Bible and the Book of Mormon. Together these four works are called the "standard works" and represent the Mormon canon of scripture. The LDS church publishes its own edition of the Bible and uses the King James Version for its translation.

  While other informal writings by Church leaders are viewed as valuable aids to understanding the Mormon faith, they are not considered canonical scripture or official Church doctrine. That is why this booklet tries to examine Mormon doctrine using, as much as possible, only citations from one of these four "standard works" and not the writings of early Mormon leaders.

- Christian churches believe that public divine revelation ceased after the death of the last apostle. But, according to their ninth article of faith, Mormons "believe all that God has revealed, all that He does now reveal, and we believe that He will yet reveal many great and important things pertaining to the Kingdom of God." Mormons believe that God can reveal new doctrine to believers through the announcements of the Church's president who is considered to be, "a prophet, having all the gifts of God which he bestows upon the head of the church."[6]

2. What are some common myths about the LDS church?

Before we examine the differences between the LDS church and the Catholic Church, we should refute some common myths about the Mormon faith:

"Mormons practice polygamy."
Mormons do not currently practice polygamy, meaning they do not enter into marriages with more than one spouse at the same time.[7] In an October 1998 General Conference, former LDS president Gordon Hinkley said, "If any of our members are found to be practicing plural marriage, they are excommunicated, the most serious penalty the church can impose."

This myth is derived from the fact that the LDS church did practice polygamy in its early years. In 1843, Joseph Smith announced that God had revealed to him that polygamy was morally acceptable. This was then recorded in Doctrine and Covenants 132:61–66. Todd Compton, who is a practicing Mormon and a professional historian, has shown that Joseph Smith had at least thirty-three wives who were unofficially "sealed" to him in marriage.[8]

In the late 1800s, the United States government outlawed polygamy and prosecuted Mormons who engaged in the practice. However, the conflict between the church and the state began to dissipate in 1890 when LDS president Wilford Woodruff claimed he received a revelation from God saying that Mormons should no longer engage in polygamy.[9]

"Mormons take part in secret rituals that involve illicit sex. They are also threatened with death if they reveal these rituals."

Mormons use temples as a place to perform their sacred rites. The three most common rituals that take place there are endowments (where Mormons learn about their faith and receive spiritual gifts); sealings (where Mormons get married); and ordinances for the dead, which are supposed to impart spiritual gifts to those who have already died.[10] Mormons consider these rituals sacred and do not discuss them outside the temple. Usually, only LDS members with cards called "Temple Recommends" that prove they are in good standing with the Church can enter a temple.

In the interest of respecting Latter-day Saints, this booklet will not reveal the temple endowment rituals, though I will say they are fairly innocuous. There are no sexual aspects to them, and members are not threatened with death if they reveal what takes place in the rituals.

"Mormons wear magic underwear."
After Mormons take part in the endowment ceremony in the temple, they receive an undergarment that must be worn "day and night" for the rest of their lives. This garment is worn under their everyday clothes and consists of a two-piece shirt and shorts that are tailored to fit either a man or a woman. The garments should always be worn but can be temporarily removed for activities that would be difficult to do while wearing them (such as swimming). According to an official LDS handbook, "The garment provides a constant reminder of the covenants made in a temple. When properly worn, it provides protection against temptation and evil. Wearing the garment is also an outward expression of an inward commitment to follow the Savior."[11]

The garment is not considered magical but sacred, and because of this Mormons do not display them publicly. The garments have a significance similar to that of the scapular, a small cloth necklace some Catholics wear to remind them of their commitment to Christ and to help them receive the graces to live out that commitment.

"Mormons aren't allowed to ingest caffeine or drink soda."
Doctrine and Covenants 89 is also called the "Words of Wisdom" and includes several dietary restrictions for Mormons. Specifically, it prohibits the consumption of wine (except for worship services), alcohol, tobacco, and "hot drinks," which Mormons consider to be coffee or tea. Although Mormons are advised to consume caffeine carefully lest they develop bad health habits, the church does not prohibit consuming caffeinated drinks that are not coffee or tea.[12]

"Mormons worship Joseph Smith."
Mormons do not worship anyone called Mormon, or the angel Moroni (who is displayed on the top of LDS temples as an angel blowing a long horn), or Joseph Smith, (although Smith is honored as a prophet). Mormons worship God the Father and believe Jesus is both the "literal Son of God" and the savior of mankind. However, the Mormon view of both God the Father and God the Son is not the same as the Christian view of those two persons, as the following answers will demonstrate.

3. What do Mormons believe about God?

In order to understand the LDS church, it is helpful to compare the Mormon worldview (how Mormons view reality as a whole) to the Catholic worldview (which is also largely shared with Protestants and Eastern Orthodox Christians). While both Mormons and Christians believe that God is "the Supreme and Absolute Being in whom we believe and whom we worship,"[13] Catholics (and other Christians) disagree with Mormons over the physical nature of God.

For example, Doctrine and Covenants 130:3 says, "The idea that the Father and the Son dwell in a man's heart is an old sectarian notion, and is false." Joseph Smith said this idea was false because God is not a spiritual being who created everything from nothing. Instead, God is a man with a flesh-and-blood body who organized preexisting matter into the shape of our universe. Since God has a physical body, he can't literally dwell in our hearts. According to Doctrines and Covenants 130:22, "The Father has a body of flesh and bones as tangible as man's."

Catholics believe, on the other hand, that God is an infinite and perfect spirit who is not confined to a physical body. In Jeremiah 23:24 God says, "Can a man hide himself in secret places so that I cannot see him? Do I not fill heaven and earth?" It's important to remember that even though God is everywhere, he is not identical to the stuff that exists everywhere. For example, you aren't literally holding a piece of God when you read this booklet. Instead, God is *transcendent*—he exists beyond space and time, since he created those things. John 1:3 says "not a single thing" was made apart from God, and Colossians 1:16 says, "[I]n him all things were created, in heaven and on earth, visible and invisible." Since God made everything, including space and time, God can't be made of what he created but must instead be *immaterial* and *eternal* (or "spaceless" and "timeless").

In fact, John 4:24 says, "God is spirit," and Jesus makes it clear in Luke 24:39 that "a spirit has not flesh and bones." The idea that God is a spirit and not a man was the common understanding of God in the early Christian church. The second-century Church father St. Irenaeus taught that God "is simple, not composed of parts, without structure, altogether like and equal to himself alone. He is all mind, all spirit."[14]

It's important to remember that, although God is a spirit, he is also all-powerful. He can do anything that is logically possible, including the act of becoming man in the Incarnation. While God can acquire a human body if he wants one, God doesn't *need* a body, and God the Father exists without one.

Finally, even though God exists beyond the universe, he is still *immanent*, equally present in every part of the universe. How is this possible? St. Thomas Aquinas said that God "was from eternity before there was any place. Yet by the immensity of His power He reaches all things that are in place."[15] God doesn't exist in a particular place, but his power and knowledge allow him to be present and active in every place.

4. How do Mormons defend the view that God has a body?

One way Mormons defend the view that God has a physical body is to quote Genesis 1:26: "Let us make man in our image, after our likeness." If we are made in God's image, shouldn't our bodies look like our heavenly Father's body? But being "made in the image of God" means only that humans have rational abilities and resemble God in an immaterial way, such as by being loving or just.[16]

The interpretation that "image and likeness" refers to immaterial qualities in man (and not physical likeness) is bolstered by Genesis 9:6: "Whoever sheds the blood of man, by man shall his blood be shed; for God made man in his own image." God doesn't condemn killing humans because they physically look like him but because they possess the immaterial qualities of having intrinsic value and God-given authority over creation.

Another LDS defense of the idea that God has a physical body like you or me points to Scripture passages that describe God sitting on a throne (Psalm 47:8), having a right hand (Acts 7:55–56), and appearing to human beings in bodily form. One example of this would be Moses seeing God's "backside" and speaking with God "face to face as a man speaks to his friend" (Exod. 33:11). Mormons say that these passages don't make sense unless God the Father has a physical body.

But we must be careful when we interpret verses that use non-literal language in order to communicate a spiritual truth about God. For example, Psalm 91:4 says God "will cover you with his feathers, and under his wings you will find refuge." But this passage teaches us about God's love for us, not his wingspan.

Are descriptions of God having a human body literal or non-literal? We should believe that the bodily descriptions of God are not literal, because reason shows us that God is the immaterial creator of the universe, and Scripture teaches that God is invisible (Colossians 1:15, 1 Timothy 1:17). 1 Timothy 6:16 says that God "dwells in unapproachable light, whom no man has ever seen or can see." When Moses spoke to God "face to face," this was merely an expression of the intimacy Moses had with God (even a blind man can speak to someone face to face). God himself told Moses, "you cannot see my face; for no one shall see me and live" (Exod. 33:20).

Even though God is by nature invisible and immaterial, he can appear to human beings under a visible form in order to reveal himself to them. He did this with Moses in the form of a burning bush (Exodus 3:1–22) and with Jacob when he took the form of a human being who wrestled with him (Genesis 32:24–32).[17] But how could people see Jesus if he was also God? The reason people in the Gospels could see Jesus was because Jesus voluntarily set aside his divine glory in order to become a man like us (Philippians 2:7). Jesus said in John 6:46, "Not that any one has seen the Father except him who is from God; he has seen the Father." In other words, no one has ever seen God except for Jesus, because Jesus is fully divine just like the Father.

While some people may find comfort in worshipping a God who has a body that resembles theirs, there is even greater comfort in knowing that God does not have a body that forces him to live billions of miles away from us (see question 5). Instead, God can live literally within us, because there is no physical place where he *has* to reside. As Jesus said in John 14:23, "If a man loves me, he will keep my word, and my Father will love him, and we will come to him and make our home with him."[18]

5. What do Mormons believe about men being able to become gods?

In a speech he gave at the funeral for elder King Follett (which is now called the King Follett sermon), Joseph Smith said, "I am going to tell you how God came to be God. We have imagined and supposed that God was God from all eternity. I will refute that idea, and take away the veil, so that you may see. . . . God himself was once as we are now, and is an exalted man, and sits enthroned in yonder heavens!"[19]

Mormons believe that God's body is actually a glorified version of the body he had when he was a human being like us. God was once a man like us, but he has been exalted and now rules from within the universe. According to the Book of Abraham (which is a part of the LDS scriptures called *The Pearl of Great Price*), God rules on a throne situated near a star or planet in our universe called Kolob. One Mormon hymn sings of Kolob in this way:

If you could hie to Kolob
In the twinkling of an eye,
And then continue onward
With that same speed to fly,
Do you think that you could ever,
Through all eternity,
Find out the generation
Where Gods began to be?[20]

Mormons believe that there is more than one God, and gods can "come to be" or begin to exist. One LDS scripture that teaches the existence of multiple gods is the Book of Abraham, which describes the creation of the world in its fourth chapter. But where Genesis uses the singular noun *God*, the Book of Abraham uses the plural noun *Gods*.[21] For example, Genesis 1:1 says, "In the beginning God created the heavens and the earth"; but Abraham 4:1 says, "And they went down at the beginning, and they, that is the Gods, organized and formed the heavens and the earth." While many people call this polytheism, most Mormons refer to this as a belief in a plurality of Gods.[22]

In regards to the doctrine that men can become gods, the fifth LDS president, Lorenzo Snow, summarized this teaching in the aphorism:

As man now is, God once was;
As God now is, man may be.

Mormons believe that God and man are of the same species. Human beings are simply less developed gods and have the potential to be "exalted" or become gods—provided they follow LDS teachings. Joseph Smith said in the King Follett sermon, "Here, then, is eternal life—to know the only wise and true God; and you have got to learn how to be gods yourselves, and to be kings and priests to God, the same as all gods have done before you, namely, by going from one small degree to another, and from a small capacity to a great one; from grace to grace, from exaltation to exaltation."

But if the God of this world was once a man, then who created him and his world? The Mormon answer is that another God created that man and his world. But since *that* God was also once a man, another God must have created him. By logical necessity, this process must continue infinitely into the past, since there could be no "final" God who himself wasn't formerly a mortal man. That is why Mormons call this cycle of men becoming gods *eternal progression*. The cycle has always taken place in the past and will always take place into the future.

Some people say that eternal progression means that when Mormons die they become gods who will rule over their own planets. Joseph Smith's successor, Brigham Young, said, "All those who are counted worthy to be exalted and to become Gods, even the sons of God, will go forth and have earths and worlds like those who framed this and millions on millions of others."[23] While some early LDS leaders like Young explicitly taught about "having worlds," the modern LDS church says this is not official doctrine and warns its members against speculating about the nature of the afterlife. One recent LDS statement on the subject says, "While few Latter-day Saints would identify with caricatures of having their own planet, most would agree that the awe inspired by creation hints at our creative potential in the eternities."[24]

While Mormons reject the crude statement, "Mormons will get their own planet in heaven," this teaching seems to imply that we will be "creators" in the next life just as our heavenly Father is our creator in this life. Since the heavenly Father watches over children who live on a planet, then why wouldn't our "creative potential in the eternities" include the same thing?

6. Why do Catholics reject the doctrine of eternal progression?

Catholicism teaches that there is an unbridgeable gap between what God is and what man is. God is the infinite creator who has always existed, always will exist, and depends on nothing in order to exist. Human beings are finite creatures that begin to exist and depend on God for everything in order to exist. Human beings can, through God's grace, become more *like* God in goodness and holiness, even to the point of becoming "perfect, as our heavenly Father is perfect."[25] But we cannot become gods or attain the abilities that are unique to God, such as being all-powerful or all-knowing. The Catholic Church holds this view for at least three reasons.

First, the doctrine of eternal progression contradicts the Christian belief in monotheism, or the belief that there is only one God. Congruous with arguments from reason (see St. Thomas Aquinas, *Summa Theologica* I.11.3), Scripture teaches there is only one God, and we are to worship him alone. Deuteronomy 4:39 says, "Know therefore this day, and lay it to your heart, that the LORD is God in heaven above and on the earth beneath; there is no other." In Isaiah 45:5, God says, "I am the Lord, and there is no other, besides me there is no God."

A LDS could object that there is indeed only one God of *this world*, but there are other Gods beyond our world. However, in Isaiah 44:8 God says, "Is there a God besides me? I know not any." If the God of this world were omniscient, then wouldn't he know about the God that he worshipped when he was a man? God also makes it clear in Isaiah 43:10 that "Before me no god was formed, nor shall there be any after me." This can't refer to false gods or idols, because many of those are still "formed" to this day. Instead, the Bible teaches that no other God besides the one true God has ever existed, and no other God ever will exist.

The New Testament also firmly teaches there is only one God. Jesus described God as "the one and only God" (John 5:44) and "the only true God" (John 17:3). St. Paul describes God as "the only wise God" (Romans 16:27) and the only being who possesses immortality (1 Timothy 6:16). St. Ignatius wrote in the early second century that the early Christians were persecuted because they "convince[d] the disobedient that there is one God, who manifested himself through his Son, Jesus Christ."[26]

The second reason Catholics reject eternal progression is because it contradicts the created and dependent nature of the world. Even if the universe were eternal, that would not explain why the universe never failed to exist at any point in the infinite past. Instead, there must be a being that can't fail to exist and keeps the entire universe in existence. This being can not possess existence as a kind of accidental feature but must instead be "existence" or "being" itself. St. Thomas Aquinas called this "necessary being" God and showed that God cannot depend on anything else in order to exist, because everything depends on *him* in order to exist.[27] This means God could never have been a finite and mortal man who depended on something else in order to exist.

Furthermore, there are scientific and philosophical reasons to believe that the entire physical universe (all of space, time, matter, and energy) began to exist from nothing.[28] In 2012 the influential and nonreligious cosmologist Alexander Vilenkin said, "All the evidence we have says that the universe had a beginning."[29] If that's true, then only an immaterial and eternal God—and not an exalted man who lives within the universe—could have brought the universe into existence from a state of nothingness.

Finally, eternal progression contradicts our understanding of God's nature. Malachi 3:6 says, "I the LORD do not change," and Psalm 90:2 says, "[F]rom everlasting to everlasting thou art God." From one infinite direction to another infinite direction, God is always God and is never anything else. God could never have been "not God," and he could never have been an imperfect, mortal human being. Numbers 23:19 says, "God is not man, that he should lie, or a son of man, that he should repent," and, in Hosea 11:9, God emphatically declares, "I am God, and not man." The

Book of Mormon even teaches that God "is unchangeable from all eternity to all eternity" (Moroni 8:18). If God were once a man, then God did change, and both the Bible and the Book of Mormon are wrong.

7. How do Mormons defend the doctrine of eternal progression?

LDS writers say we can know from revelation that there are many gods and not just one God. They may cite 1 Corinthians 8:5–6, where Paul says, "For though there be that are called gods, whether in heaven or in earth, (as there be gods many, and lords many,) but to us there is but one God, the Father, of whom are all things, and we in him; and one Lord Jesus Christ, by whom are all things, and we by him" (KJV).

But in this verse Paul is not saying there are many gods and god the Father just happens to be the one god Christians serve. That would not explain what Paul means when he says "all things" are of God the Father. How could "all things" be of God the Father if he were only one god among an infinite collection of gods? Instead, God the Father is our only God, and Jesus Christ is our only Lord, because they are the only real beings who hold those titles. The phrase "For us there is only one God" should not be taken to mean, "As for us, we worship only one God." It should be taken to mean, "As for us, we know that there is only one God."

Other passages cited by Mormons include the Psalms and John 10. Psalm 86:8 says, "There is none like you among the gods, O Lord," and Psalm 82:1 says, "God has taken his place in the divine council; in the midst of the gods he holds judgment." In John 10:31–34, Jesus confronts the Jewish leaders who accuse him of blasphemy for "making himself God." Jesus answers them by saying, "Is it not written in your law, 'I said, you are gods'?"

Did Jesus teach that there are many gods and not just one? Notice that Jesus referred to a law that read, "You *are* gods." LDS theology teaches that men can eventually progress to godhood, but it denies that mortal men can become gods prior to death. So what did Jesus mean when he said the Jewish leaders were called "gods"?

In the Bible, human rulers and judges are sometimes called "gods" (Exodus 22:9), or, in Hebrew, "elohims." Jesus quoted Psalm 82 because it criticizes human judges like the Pharisees who were unfair or wicked and fell short of the standard set by God. Psalm 82:7 says those "elohims" will "die like men," so these beings were not actual gods. Jesus' point in John 10:31–34 is that if the corrupt human leaders in Psalm 82 could be called gods, then why can't Jesus, who "the Father has sanctified and sent into the world" (John 10:36) be called God. After all, he actually is God!

Mormons also deny the traditional Christian teaching that God does not change and is not a human being.

They say that passages like Malachi 3:6, which describes God saying, "I the LORD do not change," mean only that God's character or his faithfulness to mankind will never waver. But how could a being that went from being imperfect to perfect, went from being a sinner to becoming pure goodness, and went from being mortal to being immortal not be an obvious case of something changing, even if it is just changing in character?

Mormons may also refer to paragraph 460 of the *Catechism*, which says, "The Word became flesh to make us 'partakers of the divine nature.' . . . For the Son of God became man so that we might become God. The only-begotten Son of God, wanting to make us sharers in his divinity, assumed our nature, so that he, made man, might make men gods." Now, the Catholic Church does teach that humans can, through the grace of God, acquire God's shareable (or communicable) attributes like holiness or impartiality. This is what St. Athanasius, who is quoted in paragraph 460, meant when he said, "we might become God." But St. Athanasius also said, "[W]e become by grace what God is by nature"—in other words, God gives us his divine life so that we *resemble* him but we never *become* him.[30]

Renowned historian of Christianity Jaroslav Pelikan says that the doctrine that men could become like God in holiness (what is called *theosis*) was, among people like Athanasius, "not to be viewed as analogous to classical Greek theories about the promotion of human beings to divine rank, and in that sense not to be defined by natural theology at all; on such errors they pronounced their 'Anathema!'"[31] In other words, the Church Fathers would not have recognized the Mormon doctrine of exaltation as being a variation of their doctrine of theosis. Instead, they would have considered it heresy.

8. What do Mormons believe about creation?

Catholics believe that God—who is a Trinity of Father, Son, and Holy Spirit—created all things out of nothing at some point in the distant past.[32] Hebrews 11:3 states, "[T]he worlds were prepared by the word of God, so that what is seen was made from things that are not visible" (in other translations "was not made out of visible things."). The Shepherd of Hermas, written around the year A.D. 80, says, "Believe first of all that God is one, that he created all things and set them in order and brought out of nonexistence into existence everything that is, and that he contains all things while he himself is uncontained."[33]

Mormons, on the other hand, believe that the world is eternal, and God is just one being who exists within it. God created our world in the same way that a baker "creates" a cake, by combining preexisting ingredients. Eric Shuster, a former Catholic turned Mormon, writes, "Latter-day Saint doctrine holds that the universe was *formed* and *organized*, not created *ex nihilo*, 'out of nothing' as Catholic doctrine holds. This is not an insignificant difference."[34]

According to Mormonism, not only is matter uncreated and eternal, so are the souls of human beings. Doctrine and Covenants 93:29 teaches, "Man was also in the beginning with God. Intelligence, or the light of truth, was not created or made, neither indeed can be."[35] In order to create human beings, God, whom Mormons call "Heavenly Father," first fashioned spirit bodies for these "intelligences" with the help of a Heavenly Mother. After receiving spirit bodies, we enjoyed a relationship with Heavenly Father that Mormons call our "pre-mortal existence." However, all human beings have forgotten this existence since Heavenly Father sent us to Earth in order to be born as human beings.

In 1909, the LDS church officially recognized the existence of Heavenly Mother and said, "All men and women are in the similitude of the universal Father and Mother and are literally the sons and daughters of Deity."[36] LDS writings say that the exact process of how Heavenly Father and Heavenly Mother "begat" spirit children, as well as many truths about Heavenly Mother herself, are unknown and one should not speculate on the matter.

The *Catechism* says that calling God "Father" indicates that he is the origin of all things and lovingly watches over us. It does not mean that we are biologically related to God or are his "spirit-children."[37] Only Jesus is able to call God "his" father, while we call God "our" father, because Jesus is the unique and "only son of God" (John 3:18). Human beings, on the other hand, are God's children by *adoption*, because we are not of the same species as God (unlike Jesus, who is fully divine). Romans 8:15 makes this clear when it says that with a "spirit of adoption" we can call God "Abba" or "Daddy."

Finally, Mormons defend their belief that we existed with God as "spirit-children" before our conception by appealing to Scripture passages that speak of God knowing or choosing people before they existed. These include Jeremiah 1:5 ("Before I formed you in the womb I knew you") and Ephesians 1:4 ("he chose us in him before the foundation of the world"). But these passages refer to *ideal* preexistence, or something existing as an idea in God's mind before it exists in reality. Jeremiah 1:5 does not describe Jeremiah knowing God and Ephesians 1:4 does not say we rejoiced at being chosen, since neither Jeremiah nor we existed prior to the creation. Jesus Christ is the only person who had an *actual* preexistence with the Father before his earthly birth. This is confirmed in John 17:5 when Jesus asks the Father to "glorify me in your own presence with the glory that I had in your presence *before the world existed.*" The Bible never speaks of human beings having this kind of existence with God before they are conceived.

9. What do Mormons believe about Jesus Christ?

Mormons believe that Jesus was once an "intelligence" like us who existed from eternity past. He was not always divine, and he was not always the Son of God. Instead, God chose Jesus to become "the first-born" among the intelligences by giving him the first spirit body. Doctrine and Covenants 93:31–33 describes Jesus telling Joseph Smith, "I was in the beginning with the Father, and am the First-born; And all those who are begotten through me are partakers of the glory of the same, and are the church of the First-born. Ye were also in the beginning with the Father; that which is Spirit, even the Spirit of truth."

In 1909, the First Presidency released a statement that said, "The Father of Jesus is our Father also. . . . Jesus, however, is the first-born among all the sons of God—the first begotten in the spirit, and the only begotten in the flesh. He is our elder brother, and we, like Him, are in the image of God."[38] The "only begotten in the flesh" means that Jesus has the distinction of being the only human being who was begotten by Heavenly Father. Whereas LDS leaders like Brigham Young taught that Jesus was "begotten of his Father, as we were of our fathers," or through sexual intercourse with Mary, the modern LDS church does not take a position on how Jesus became incarnate.[39] However, it denies that positions like Young's were ever taught as official Mormon doctrine.

One of the interesting consequences of the Mormon view of Jesus is that Jesus is not only our brother, he is also the brother of Heavenly Father's other spirit children, which includes the fallen angel Lucifer. In response to the oft-repeated charge, "Mormons believe that Jesus and the Devil are brothers," Mormon writers are quick to point out that this belief does not mean that Jesus and Satan deserve the same respect, are similar in status, or that Mormons worship Satan. It means simply that we (along with Jesus) are all God's spirit children. But as one LDS apologetics website admits, "[I]t is technically true to say that Jesus and Satan are 'brothers,' in the sense that both have the same spiritual parent, God the Father."[40]

Some Mormons defend the belief that Jesus is our "eldest brother" by citing Scripture passages that describe Jesus as "the first-born among many brethren" (Romans 8:29) and the "first-born of creation" (Colossians 1:15). But this does not take into account that the term *first-born* doesn't always mean "the oldest within a family." In Exodus 4:22, God said that the nation of Israel was his "first-born," even though Israel was not the first nation to come into existence. Instead, Israel simply held a place of favor with God among all the nations. Likewise, in Psalm 89:27, God said of David, "I will make him the first-born, the highest of the kings of the earth," but David was not the first king to ever reign. He instead had a position of preeminence over all other kings.

Catholics believe in a similar way that Jesus' title "first-born of creation" means he has authority over all of creation, not that he was the first created thing. After all, Colossians 1:15–17 says that through Jesus *all things* were created, Jesus is before *all things*, and in Jesus *all things* hold together. Clearly, in order to be before all things and to have created all things, Jesus can't be one of the things that was created. Instead, Jesus must be co-equal and co-eternal with the Father, who also created those things. Jesus is not one of the Father's "spirit-children" but is instead the uncreated and eternal Son of God who created the world alongside the Father.

Finally, "first-born among many brethren" in Romans 8:29 means that Jesus was the first human to take part in the glory of the resurrection—not that Jesus was the oldest of God's created spirit children. That verse says that God planned for others to be "conformed" to Christ's image, becoming his brethren by sharing in the future glory that he received first.

10. What is the Catholic view of Jesus?

Jesus existed as God the Son from eternity, but for our sake he became man and acquired a human nature. Since his Incarnation, Jesus is fully God and fully man—one divine person with two natures, one that is fully human and one that is fully divine.[41] There was never a time when the Son did not exist, was not the Son, or was not as divine as the Father.[42]

John 1:1 says, "In the beginning was the Word, and the Word was with God, and the Word was God." The Word was not an "intelligence," a "spirit-child," or "a god," but simply God. We know the Word is God the Son, because John 1:14 says the Word became flesh and dwelt among us. Jesus says in Revelation 22:13, "I am the Alpha and the Omega, the first and the last, the beginning and the end." Jesus is not simply one more god in an infinite line of gods. He is instead the one true God we worship, with the Father and the Holy Spirit. These three divine persons are not three gods who possess different levels of glory but one true God who exists as three co-equal and co-eternal persons (see question 11).

Some Mormons say that Jesus is not fully divine as is the Father, because in John 14:28 Jesus says, "The Father is greater than I." But in this verse Jesus means that the Father is greater than him in *position*, not *divinity*. Christ was "lesser" in this setting because he humbly set aside his divine glory in order to become a man (Philippians 2:7). During his earthly life, Jesus was "a little lower than the angels" (Hebrews 2:7); but after his Resurrection, Jesus was given "the name which is above all other names" (Philippians 2:9), a title that belongs to God alone.

Since Latter-day Saints believe Jesus is merely "a god" who is closer to our level of existence than

Heavenly Father's, they do not pray to Jesus. But when they are asked why they don't pray to Jesus, most Mormons will say something like, "Jesus taught his disciples to address their prayers to 'our Father,' and Jesus told his disciples to 'ask of the Father in my name.' Jesus never told us to pray to him."

But because Jesus gave us one way to pray does not mean it is the only way we are to pray. For example, Mormons give thanks to Heavenly Father in their prayers, even though Jesus never showed his followers how to give thanks to God when they pray. It seems more likely that Mormons pray to the Father alone because they are following the prescription in the Book of Mormon where Jesus says, "[Y]e must always pray unto the Father in my name" (3 Nephi 18:19).

However, the Bible gives us many examples of praying to and worshipping Jesus as the almighty and only God. After his Resurrection, Jesus received worship from his disciples (Matthew 28:9) and Thomas called Jesus "My Lord and my God" (John 20:28). Before he was martyred, St. Stephen prayed to the ascended Jesus, "Lord Jesus, receive my spirit." St. Paul said, "[M]ay our Lord Jesus Christ himself and God our Father . . . comfort your hearts and strengthen them in every good work and word" (2 Thess. 2:16–17). Notice that Paul does not ask the Father "in Jesus name" to comfort believers but petitions *both* the Father and the Son, which implies they are equals. If the apostle

Thomas can confidently say to Jesus "My Lord and my God," Stephen can ask Jesus to receive his spirit, and Paul can ask Christ to comfort us, why shouldn't we ask Jesus to hear and answer our prayers?

11. Is the Church of Jesus Christ of Latter-day Saints a Christian Church?

Just as anyone who worships the God of Islam is a Muslim, a Christian is anyone who worships the God of Christianity. Since Mormons believe in the existence of many gods, that God the Father was once a man, and that Jesus and the Holy Spirit are not fully divine, it follows that they do not worship the God of Christianity, and so Mormons are not Christians. Christians believe that there is only one God, but they also believe that the Father is God, the Son is God (John 1:1, John 8:58, John 20:28, Romans 9:5, Titus 2:13), and the Holy Spirit is God (Acts 5:1–4). These texts don't say Jesus or the Holy Spirit are gods, but that they are *God*. The only way all these statements can be true is if God is not zero persons (like a rock) or one person (like you or me) but in his infinite majesty is three persons: Father, Son, and Holy Spirit.

While the Trinity may not be easy to understand, who are we to limit the all-powerful God and say how many persons he can be while still remaining one God? In fact, most LDS attacks on the Trinity stem from misunderstandings of it, such as when Joseph Smith said, "[T]hree in one, and one in three! It is a curious organization. . . . All are to be crammed into one God, according to sectarianism. It would make the biggest God in all the world. He would be a wonderfully big God—he would be a giant or a monster."[43] But each person of the Trinity is not a *part* of God. Instead, each member *is God*, and because of this each member of the Holy Trinity deserves the same level of worship as God.

A Christian is someone who is as comfortable petitioning Jesus Christ to "have mercy on me" or the Holy Spirit to "fill the hearts of your faithful" as he is comfortable asking the Father to "give us this day our daily bread," since all three of these persons are God. Although Mormons claim that they, too, believe in "one God," what they mean is that they believe in one *collection* of Gods. For Mormons, the Father, Son, and Holy Spirit (the latter of whom Mormons call "the Holy Ghost") are three Gods who cooperate so perfectly they might as well be one God. But this is like saying that a perfectly cooperating baseball team has but one player.

In Matthew 28:19, Jesus says to baptize in the *name* of the Father, Son, and Holy Spirit, not in the *names* of these persons. This implies that, even though he is three persons, God is still one being. While the Catholic Church recognizes baptisms performed by other Christians that use the proper baptismal formula, it does not recognize LDS baptisms. Even though Mormons use the proper baptismal formula (i.e., they refer to the Father, Son, and Holy Spirit) they don't mean what Christians mean by those terms—three co-eternal and co-equal divine persons. They mean instead two spirit children (the Son and Holy Spirit) who were made divine by a Father who himself used to be a human being and was exalted to godhood by another god.

Most Mormons bristle at the suggestion that they are not Christians, but in saying this Catholics don't mean Mormons are bad people. We simply mean that, unlike Catholics, Protestants, and the Eastern Orthodox churches, Mormons do not worship the god of Christianity, who is the only God and exists as three co-equal and co-eternal persons. Fr. Luis Ladaria, in an article published in the August 2001 edition of the Vatican newspaper L'Osservatore Romano, said the differences between Mormonism and Christianity are so great that "one cannot even consider that this [Mormon] doctrine is a heresy. . . . The teaching of the Mormons has a completely different matrix."

Of course, Mormons may say that they do worship the God of Christianity, and it is the Catholics, Protestants, and other "Christians" who are wrong about what God is like. That could be the case, but now we must examine the authority of the LDS church to make such a bold claim. Why should we believe the Mormon interpretation of the Bible is correct and its doctrines about God are true? Why should we believe that God founded the LDS church? Mormonism's authority rests on its founder's claim of being a prophet and having received divine revelation. One way to see if Joseph Smith was a prophet of God is to examine one of the revelations Smith claimed God gave him: the Book of Mormon.

12. What is the Book of Mormon?

According to Joseph Smith, in 1823, an angel named Moroni appeared to him and revealed the location of a set of gold plates inscribed in a language Smith called "reformed Egyptian." Smith met with Moroni over a period of four years to prepare to translate the plates, which Smith allegedly accomplished by peering inside of a hat and using a set of seer stones to illuminate the reformed Egyptian characters on the plates. Smith would then dictate the translation he saw to a scribe.[44]

In 1828, a wealthy farmer named Martin Harris offered to assist Smith in the translation process, but Harris lost 116 pages of the translated manuscript Smith gave him. Smith claimed that God was angry at the loss of the pages and would now allow Smith only to translate from another set of golden plates. These plates told the same story as the original plates but from a slightly different perspective.

Of course, if Smith were just dictating the story from memory and not actually translating, it would have been nearly impossible for him to reproduce what he originally dictated to Harris and prove he was a prophet. Smith himself even describes in Doctrine and Covenants 10 how his critics would have used the loss of the pages to try and prove that he was not actually translating the golden plates but reciting a story from memory. Despite these challenges, in 1829 a schoolteacher named Oliver Cowdery helped Smith finish his translation, and on March 26, 1830, the Book of Mormon was published.

The book follows the descendants of Lehi, a righteous man living at the time of the prophet Jeremiah, who traveled with his family from Jerusalem across the Atlantic Ocean to the Americas. The Book of Mormon is divided into chapters based on the allegedly different authors who recorded the history of Lehi's descendants. The two primary lines of Lehi were the Nephites and the Lamanites, both of whom built elaborate cities and engaged in several massive and violent wars with each other. The high point of the Book of Mormon takes place in 3rd Nephi, when Jesus appears to the Nephites shortly after his Resurrection and preaches the gospel to them.

The book concludes with the testimony of Moroni, who was the only Nephite to survive a final battle with the Lamanites in the fifth century (the Lamanites then became the ancestors of modern Native Americans).[45] Before he died, Moroni gathered the golden plates that recorded the history of his people and buried them on a hillside. After his death, Moroni became an angel and later revealed to Joseph Smith the location of the plates (which turned out to be in upstate New York).

Most of the arguments Mormons offer in defense of the authenticity of the Book of Mormon are variants of the following four:

The argument from witnesses

No one can presently verify the authenticity of the golden plates, because an angel allegedly took them back to heaven after they were translated.[46] However, the opening pages of the Book of Mormon record the testimony of three witnesses—Martin Harris, Oliver Cowdery, and David Whitmer—who claimed to have seen the plates. The Book of Mormon also includes the testimony of eight other witnesses who handled the plates.

The argument from author incapability

Mormons often claim that Joseph Smith could not have created the Book of Mormon, because he was not educated enough to write such a long and detailed work. They point to letters in which Smith writes things about his childhood such as, "I was merely instructed in reading, writing, and the ground rules of arithmetic."[47]

The argument from biblical prophecy

Mormons sometimes quote verses from the Bible that they say predict God's revelation in the Book of Mormon. One example of this is Ezekiel 37:16–17: "Mortal, take a stick and write on it, 'For Judah, and the Israelites associated with it'; then take another stick and write on it, 'For Joseph (the stick of Ephraim) and all the house of Israel associated with it'; and join them together into one stick, so that they may become one in your hand." Mormons claim the Bible represents the stick of Judah and the Book of Mormon represents the stick of Ephraim, and the two are finally united in the LDS faith.[48]

The argument from the Holy Spirit

When LDS missionaries present the Book of Mormon to potential converts, they often ask them to read the book, or certain excerpts, and then ask God to confirm in their hearts that the Book of Mormon is true. The missionaries usually appeal to James 1:5: "If any of you is lacking in wisdom, ask God, who gives to all generously and ungrudgingly, and it will be given you."

13. Why don't Catholics accept the arguments made on behalf of the Book of Mormon?

Let's examine each:

The argument from witnesses

Even if the witnesses were telling the truth, all they confirm is the existence of golden-looking plates. The plates could have been natural artifacts or even forgeries. There's no reason to conclude that the plates were ancient artifacts that contained the contents of the modern Book of Mormon.

We have reason to doubt the witnesses' testimonies. Joseph Smith's *History of the Church* describes how the first three witnesses had to pray ecstatically in order to have enough "faith" to see the plates. Mormon historian Marvin Hill writes, "[T]here is a possibility that the three witnesses saw the plates in vision only."[49] The other eight witnesses also describe only seeing or "hefting" the plates while the plates were wrapped in cloth.

All eleven witnesses were Smith's friends, family members, or financial backers. By the time of Smith's death, two of the witnesses had died and the rest had been excommunicated from the church. This stands in sharp contrast to the witnesses of the risen Jesus, who include a former enemy of the Church (St. Paul) and the apostles who remained faithful to Christ until their deaths (usually as martyrs).

The argument from author incapability

First, if this argument proves anything, it's only that Smith did not write the Book of Mormon, not that it was written by ancient Americans. It's possible a contemporary of Smith helped him write the book.[50] Second, there is no reason to think that Smith was an incompetent storyteller. His mother, Lucy Smith, said that when Smith was younger he could often deliver "the most amusing recitals" about ancient Native

Americans in such detail that it seemed that Smith had "spent his whole life with them."[51]

Furthermore, the text of the Book of Mormon bears many of the earmarks of an improvised dictation, especially the repetition of the phrase "it came to pass," which is used nearly 1,500 times.[52] Concerning the claim Smith was too uneducated to come up with the book's story, Smith's own testimony says that he spent four years meeting with the angel Moroni before he began to dictate the Book of Mormon.[53] This would have given him plenty of time to do research for his later dictation of the book.

In fact, much of the Book of Mormon's plot may have come from another book called *A View of the Hebrews* that was published five years before the Book of Mormon. Like the Book of Mormon, this book describes a group of ancient Jews who sailed to America and became the forebears of Native Americans. Even Mormon apologist B.H. Roberts admitted that *A View of the Hebrews* could have served as an inspiration for the Book of Mormon.[54]

The argument from biblical prophecy
Despite what some Mormons say, the Hebrew word for *stick* in Ezekiel 37:16–17 does not mean scroll or book. It just means *stick*, as in 1 Kings 17:12 when the widow of Zarephath was gathering sticks outside the city gates. Ezekiel 37:20–23 reveals the plain meaning of the sticks: they symbolize the reunification of the northern and

southern kingdoms of Israel, not the unification of the Bible and the Book of Mormon.

The argument from the Holy Spirit

The main problem with this argument is that it makes truth a matter of subjective feeling. Jeremiah 17:9 says, "The heart is devious above all else; it is perverse—who can understand it?" Since our feelings can cause us to fall into error, a Catholic should trust the authority of the Church and the testimony of Scripture, neither of which confirms the claims of the LDS church. A Catholic could also use this same argument to defend his testimony that the Catholic Church is true and the Book of Mormon is false.

In regards to James 1:5, this verse promises only that God will help us be *wise*, or apply our knowledge in prudent ways. It does not teach that God will give us knowledge about other religions or confirm if they are true or false. Instead, God has given us something stronger to rely on for that kind of truth. 1 Timothy 3:15 says that "the pillar and foundation of truth" is not a personal testimony but "the Church of the living God."

14. What are some other reasons that Catholics do not accept the authenticity of the Book of Mormon?

In 1 Thessalonians 5:21, St. Paul urges Christians, "Test everything, retain what is good." When Catholics and other Christians are presented with the Book of Mormon and its claim to being "another testament of Jesus Christ," they understand the need to test this amazing claim. Indeed, Catholics know that no new public revelation has been given to the Church since the death of the last apostle.[55] But even if one were nonreligious and had no belief about the nature of God's revelation to man, there would still be compelling reasons to think the Book of Mormon is not a historical work.

Lack of archaeological confirmation
Most Bibles contain maps that describe where important biblical events took place. You can visit the ruins of cities described in the Bible. The same is not true for the Book of Mormon. The Book itself contains no maps and no references to where the events it describes took place. None of the sites described in the Book of Mormon have ever been found, and even LDS scholars don't agree on the general location of where the events in the book took place.

According to the National Geographic Society, "Archaeologists and other scholars have long probed the hemisphere's past, and the society does not know of anything found so far that has substantiated the Book of Mormon."[56] While it is possible the evidence for the events in the Book of Mormon lies deep underground waiting to be discovered, this lack of evidence does not bode well for the book's claims to being historical.[57]

The existence of anachronisms

The Book of Mormon describes many things that did not exist in the Americas during the time when the events in the Book of Mormon allegedly took place. These include animals (dogs, horses, cows, elephants) plants (barley and wheat), fabrics (silk), metals (steel and iron) and technologies (swords and chariots). While it is possible, in the barest sense of the term, that these items are waiting to be discovered by archaeologists or that these modern words refer to completely different things (such as when Europeans used the term "water horse" to describe a hippopotamus) it's more likely that these anachronisms are evidence of Smith's lack of knowledge about ancient America and more proof that the Book of Mormon is a work of fiction.

Evidence of plagiarism

Significant portions of the Book of Mormon consist of a word-for-word copy of the King James Version of the Bible. These include dozens of whole chapters from the prophet Isaiah as well as scores of verses from the New Testament. Especially troubling are passages like Moroni 7:44–47 that copy large portions of the New Testament but do not cite those passages. Since the New Testament wasn't available for the Nephites to copy and place in their own records, these passages most likely came from Smith's recollection of the Bible.

In fact, in his defense of the Book of Mormon, Robert Bennett says that it is unlikely God inspired both Paul and Mormon (one of the alleged authors of a chapter in the Book of Mormon) to use the same words in their writings. He is also skeptical that they both quoted from a common source. He concludes that Joseph Smith "inadvertently slipped into language with which he was familiar," though Bennett concedes that this solution abandons the view that Smith simply wrote down what the seer stones revealed to him as he translated the Book of Mormon.[58]

15. What is the Book of Abraham?

The Book of Abraham is a translation Joseph Smith made of an ancient Egyptian papyrus that he purchased in Kirtland, Ohio, in 1830. The book claims to have been written by Abraham himself and describes his journey from Canaan to Egypt. In the latter part of the book Abraham receives a vision from God that teaches him about the existence of pre-mortal spirits, the plurality of gods, and the council of gods meeting before the creation of the world. Smith completed his translation of the book in 1835 and the full text was published in 1842. In 1880 the book became a part of the Mormon canon of Scripture.

What makes this document of interest to non-Mormons is that it includes three reproductions, or facsimiles, of the original papyri Smith translated. In the latter part of the nineteenth century, several Egyptologists examined the facsimiles and concluded that Smith's translation of them was completely wrong.[59] In 1913 the LDS church responded to criticisms of Smith's translation by saying that such criticisms didn't tell the whole story. They argued that the critics were only able to judge Smith's translations based on the *facsimiles* of the papyri, which were a small part of the originals. Perhaps the translation was accurate if one looked at the entire context of the original documents that Smith possessed.

While the papyri Smith translated were thought to have been destroyed in the Great Chicago Fire of 1871, they were rediscovered in New York City's Metropolitan Museum of Art in 1966. Both non-LDS and LDS Egyptologists have examined these original documents and concluded that the papyri Smith translated have nothing to do with Abraham and are simply ancient Egyptian funerary texts. The text itself was probably buried with an Egyptian priest named Horus and has been dated to the second century B.C., more than 1,000 years after Abraham lived. The figure that Smith claimed was Abraham in the papyri is actually the Egyptian god Osiris, and the figure he thought was Pharaoh is the Egyptian god Isis.

Mormon apologists have proposed numerous explanations for the discrepancy between what the papyri say and what Smith published in the Book of Abraham. Some have said that Smith didn't actually translate the papyri but received the contents of the Book of Abraham from God in a vision. The papyri only served as scenes that *resemble* what God showed Smith, even if their meaning has nothing to do with what God revealed. But this approach is untenable, because Smith says in his diary that he *translated* the original Egyptian of the papyri. He makes no mention of learning about the Book of Abraham through revelation.[60]

Other Mormon scholars claim that the original papyri may be incomplete and that the lost portions of the papyri could be the sections that contain the Book of Abraham. But the vast majority of the scroll Smith translated has been found, and the missing fragments would yield only a few extra details, not the full contents of the Book of Abraham. Besides, it wouldn't make sense for the missing fragments to diverge from the ordinary funeral rites present in the scroll and turn into a narrative about the patriarch Abraham.

In conclusion, the Bible says that the difference between a true prophet and a false prophet is that a true prophet's message will come to pass and he will not lead people to "worship other Gods."[61] On both of these counts Joseph Smith fails the test of being a prophet. Not only does the Book of Abraham encourage belief in the existence of other gods, its message has not come to pass. The evidence that Smith did not translate the

Book of Abraham from Egyptian papyri as he said he did is overwhelming and needs to be addressed by anyone who claims that Smith was a prophet.

16. What do Mormons believe about marriage?

While Catholics and Mormons agree that marriage is a sacred, lifelong bond between one man and one woman, they disagree over when this bond ends. The Catholic Church's canon law states that a valid, consummated marriage between two baptized persons can be dissolved only by death.[62] This is affirmed in Romans 7:1–3, which teaches that when a spouse dies the other spouse is free to remarry.

But according to the LDS church, marriage is an *eternal* reality. Any marriage sealed in an LDS temple is considered a "celestial marriage" that will last for all eternity (Mormons who are married outside of a temple have only lifelong marriages that are dissolved upon death). As one LDS statement put it, "The divine plan of happiness enables family relationships to be perpetuated beyond the grave. Sacred ordinances and covenants available in holy temples make it possible for individuals to return to the presence of God and for families to be united eternally."[63] One interesting consequence of this view is that LDS celestial marriages can be polygamous. According to one LDS manual of instructions, while a man can remarry in the temple after his wife dies (and thus have more than one spouse in heaven), a woman can be married in the temple only once.[64]

Doctrine and Covenants 131 states, "In the celestial glory there are three heavens or degrees; And in order to obtain the highest, a man must enter into this order of the priesthood [meaning the new and everlasting covenant of marriage]; And if he does not, he cannot obtain it. He may enter into the other, but that is the end of his kingdom; he cannot have an increase." Most Mormons say this teaching means that people cannot attain exaltation, or "godhood," unless they are sealed in an eternal marriage, but some Mormon writers have said that God in his mercy can grant individuals exaltation if they are unmarried through no fault of their own. What is known is that those Mormons who do marry in the proper temple ceremony will, according to Doctrine and Covenants 132:20, "be gods, because they have no end; therefore shall they be from everlasting to everlasting, because they continue; then shall they be above all, because all things are subject unto them."

The primary objection to this view of marriage is found in Mark 12:25 (and the corresponding passages in Matthew 22 and Luke 20). In these passages Jesus is speaking with the Sadducees, who denied the resurrection of the body. They posed a dilemma to Jesus about a woman who was consecutively married to seven men who all died in her lifetime. They ask

Jesus, "Whose wife will she be in the resurrection?" Christ answers that "in the resurrection they neither marry nor are given in marriage, but are like angels in heaven." The Church teaches that this means marriage does not continue in the next life, when we will be like angels, who do not engage in sexual relationships. LDS apologists, on the other hand, say that Jesus meant only that after death Christians do not *get* married. However, marriages that take place before death can continue on into the next life. But this doesn't answer the Sadducee's question: To whom was this woman married in the resurrection?

Mormons are forced to say, "None of them, because this woman apparently wasn't properly sealed in the temple to any of the men." But there is no hint of this reply in Jesus' answer. The Sadducees mistakenly think that the resurrected life is a mere continuation of earthly life, when it is really a glorified fulfillment of this life. Instead of focusing on procreation we will be focused on adoration, eternally worshipping the one true God.

17. What is the Mormon view of salvation?

According to Mormonism, in the beginning Heavenly Father sent the pre-incarnate Jesus (whose name at that time was Jehovah) and the archangel Michael to form our world from pre-existing matter. They did so and, as Doctrine and Covenants 27:11 describes, the archangel Michael became Adam (although when Adam awoke he forgot about his life as an archangel). God then created Eve, and Satan then tempted Adam and Eve to eat of the tree of knowledge of good and evil. After eating the fruit and disobeying God, Adam and Eve became mortal and could die. But Mormons believe this was a fall "upward" and a necessary part of God's plan, because prior to the fall, Adam and Eve could not have children.[65]

However, the Bible portrays the fall in negative terms. As St. Paul said, "just as by the one man's disobedience the many were made sinners, so by the one man's obedience the many will be made righteous."[66] The fall was not needed to help humans reproduce, as Mormons claim. In Genesis 1:28–29 God tells Adam and Eve before the fall to "be fruitful and multiply," which implies that they could have children (or else such a command would be pointless).

Mormons also believe that after death all souls will be given an opportunity to hear the gospel and choose Christ if they did not do so in this life.[67] Those who continue to reject Christ will suffer in a hell-like state until the final resurrection. At that event, those souls who followed the LDS "ordinances," such as receiving the temple endowment and being sealed in a temple marriage, will live eternally with God in the highest celestial kingdom. Some will even be exalted and become gods just like Heavenly Father. The remainder of humanity will dwell in either the lower *telestial* kingdom or the lowest *terrestial* kingdom, where God does not reign but the ministry of the Holy Ghost is present. Fortunately, even in these kingdoms there is a glory that "surpasses all understanding."[68] Only a very few beings, such as the Devil and his angels, will live forever in an eternal hell, or what Mormons call "the outer darkness."[69]

This contradicts the Christian understanding that it is appointed for men to die once and then be judged (Hebrews 9:27), which means one cannot accept the gospel after death. In regards to who will be in hell, Jesus frequently warns the crowds that eternal hell is not just a place for the devil or demons. He says in Matthew 7:21 that many who call him "Lord" will be told to "depart from him," and those human beings who do not love the least of their brethren "will go away into eternal punishment, but the righteous into eternal life" (Matthew 25:46). Jesus chose not to reveal the exact number of humans who will be in hell but simply gave us this sound advice about heaven: "Strive to enter" (Luke 13:24).

The third article of LDS faith states, "[T]hrough the Atonement of Christ, all mankind may be saved, by obedience to the laws and ordinances of the Gospel." According to the Book of Mormon, "[W]e know that it is by grace that we are saved, after all we can do" (2 Nephi 25:23). The Catholic Church does not teach that our works earn our salvation, and it certainly does not teach, as the Book of Mormon does, that we are saved by grace "after all we can do." "All we can do" is never enough to earn us anything from God.

However, the Catholic Church does not teach the view that we are saved by faith alone (which is the common Protestant view of salvation). Instead, when we are baptized we become an adopted child of God, and through baptism God's grace is infused into our souls and cleanses us of original sin. Throughout our lives we must continue to seek God's sanctifying grace in the sacraments and avoid mortal sin, which separates us from God (1 John 5:16–17). Since we are children of God, our good works do not *earn* our salvation, but they do *merit* it; when we do good works, God bestows on us eternal life (Rom. 2:6-7), because as God's children our works genuinely please him. But it's important to remember that our works mean nothing without God's grace working through us, and we receive God's grace through the sacraments he gave us.

One of the most important sacraments is the Eucharist, in which Catholics receive Jesus' body and blood under the form of bread and wine. It is only through this sacrament that we can obey Jesus' command in John 6:53–57, "Very truly, I tell you, unless you eat the flesh of the Son of Man and drink his blood, you have no life in you. Those who eat my flesh and drink my blood have eternal life, and I will raise them up on the last day; for my flesh is true food and my blood is true drink. Those who eat my flesh and drink my blood abide in me, and I in them."

18. What is the Great Apostasy?

At the end of the day, the issue of Catholic doctrine versus Mormon doctrine comes down to one issue: authority. Who has the authority to interpret the Bible or to even declare which individual books belong in the Bible? Who has the authority to say their interpretation of the Bible and pronouncement of Christian doctrines are correct? Catholics and Mormons agree that Christ intended to found a visible, authoritative Church that contained a particular hierarchy. Catholics and Mormons disagree, however, about the fate of the Church Jesus founded.

Mormons believe that, shortly after the time of the apostles, there was a massive falling away from the faith, or a "great apostasy." The Church became corrupted by pagan influences and ceased to have the authority to ordain priests and administer the sacraments. The Book of Mormon even describes the post-apostolic Church as "the great and abominable Church" that "took away the plain and precious parts of scripture" and "persecutes the saints of God."[70]

Catholics, on the other hand, do not believe such an event took place and trust Jesus when he said, "I will not leave you desolate" (John 14:18). They believe that the Catholic Church is the custodian of God's revelation and that Christ would never allow this custodian to perish or cease to have his authority. In order for their authority to exist for all generations, the apostles were able to transmit it to worthy successors, who we know today as the bishops and the pope. This line of authority can be traced all the way back to the twelve apostles and the chief apostle, Peter, who was the first pope. Acts 1:20 describes how the apostles could pass on their authority to future bishops, and Matthew 16:18 describes how Jesus built the Church upon the apostle Peter. The LDS church can't rightfully claim to be Christ's "true church" unless it can prove that the Church Jesus founded "fell away" or lost its authority.

But is there any evidence for this "great apostasy?" Mormons usually appeal to three types of evidence in defense of the claim that the early post-apostolic Church rebelled against the apostles' teachings and fell away from the Faith.

Old Testament prophecy
According to the prophet Amos, the days will come when people will seek across the whole Earth but not find God (Amos 8:11–12). The prophet Isaiah said that the people of God will break the "everlasting covenant" (Isaiah 24:5), and their hearts will be far from God (Isaiah 29:13).

New Testament prophecy

The apostle Paul says that, even when he was alive, there were false prophets pretending to be apostles (2 Corinthians 11:13–15) who perverted the gospel (Galatians 1:6–7). Paul laments that all the Christians in Asia turned away from him (2 Timothy 1:13–15) and in 2 Thessalonians 2:2–3 Paul warns his audience, "[T]he day of the Lord is already here. Let no one deceive you in any way; for that day will not come unless *the rebellion* (or in Greek *apostasia*) comes first, and the lawless one is revealed, the one destined for destruction."

Early Church evidence

Clement of Rome wrote in A.D. 96, "[E]very one abandons the fear of God, and is become blind in his faith, neither walks in the ordinances of his appointment, nor acts a part becoming a Christian, but walks after his own wicked lusts."[71] St. Ignatius allegedly said that in the second century he was "the last of the faithful" in the city of Antioch.[72]

We'll examine this evidence in a moment, but first let's take a look at one general reason Mormons give to support the claim that the Church fell into a total apostasy. LDS missionaries usually say that the apostasy occurred because the Church introduced "man-made ordinances" into its doctrines and practices. But, if the Church has Christ's authority, there is no problem with her changing minor traditions (such as how the Mass is performed or what vestments priests wear) just as the LDS church has the authority to change its own ordinances.

Mormons often tell Protestants that they too must believe there was a total apostasy, because if there had not been one, why didn't the Reformers reform Christ's Church instead of starting new ones?[73] They say that if the Catholic Church is not the true church, a total apostasy did occur. But this argument can be reversed. Specifically, if the total apostasy did not occur, then the Catholic Church *is* Christ's true church. So was there a total apostasy? Let's examine the LDS evidence for the total or universal apostasy, as well as the Catholic evidence for the claim that such an apostasy could never have occurred.

19. Does the Catholic Church have the authority Christ gave to the apostles?

The major flaw with all of the previous evidence for a total apostasy is that at most it shows only that *some* members of the Church fell away from the Faith. This happens in all religions, including Mormonism. As we saw earlier, the majority of the original witnesses to the Book of Mormon apostatized, but modern Mormons would not accept this fact as evidence that the *entire* LDS church fell into apostasy. When it comes to the Catholic Church, what Mormons need to show is that there was a *total* or *universal* falling away from the Faith in the first century. The evidence does not support this conclusion.

For example, the passages cited of the Old Testament refer to the Israelites abandoning their covenant with God, not the eventual falling away of Christians in the New Covenant. These passages don't even speak of an entire apostasy in Israel, because in Amos 9:8 God says he "will not utterly destroy the house of Jacob." The passages in the New Testament and the apostolic Fathers refer to people rejecting Christ's church, but none of them refers to a total apostasy. Every passage refers to *some* who would fall away (e.g. 1 Timothy 1:6 and 1 Timothy 4:1) or *some* who would be false prophets. But none of these passages claims that the entire Church would fall away or that every bishop would be replaced with a false prophet.

For example, in 2 Timothy 1:15 Paul laments how the Christians in Asia (not the continent of Asia but a small area called Asia Minor) turned away from *him*, not Christ. Paul is saddened that these Christians did not come to his aid when he was placed under arrest, not that a total apostasy has taken place. In regards to 2 Thessalonians 2:2–3, Paul is speaking of events that will take place at the Second Coming of Christ. There will be people who will rebel against God, but in 1 Thessalonians 4:17 Paul says there will still be faithful Christians who will be caught up to the Lord at the Second Coming. So, once again, there is no evidence that Paul believed the Church was teetering on the brink of failure.

Similarly, the letters of Clement and Ignatius contain admonitions against *some* people who have fallen away, such as certain members of the Church in Corinth. But Clement also reminds his readers that Jesus foresaw there would be trials for the Church and took steps to keep these trials from destroying it. He writes in A.D. 96, "Our apostles knew through our Lord Jesus Christ that there would be strife for the office of bishop. For this reason, therefore, having received perfect foreknowledge, they appointed those who have already been mentioned and afterwards added the further provision that, if they should die, other approved men should succeed to their ministry."[74]

Interestingly, when Mormons cite Galatians 1:6–7 as evidence of the apostasy, they usually neglect to mention Paul's warning in verse eight: "[E]ven if we or an *angel from heaven* should proclaim to you a gospel contrary to what we proclaimed to you, let that one be accursed!" The fact that the angel Moroni allegedly gave Joseph Smith his "Gospel" in the form of the Book of Mormon should cause concern.

Finally, along with the lack of evidence that a total apostasy took place, there is positive evidence that such an apostasy could never have taken place. In Matthew 16:18, Jesus tells Peter, "I tell you, you are Peter, and on this rock I will build my church, and the gates of Hades will not prevail against it." LDS apologists claim this means that the Church would never go out of existence permanently, but it could still go out of existence and then be restored by someone like Joseph Smith. But this position is implausible, because in Matthew 28:20, Jesus says, "I am with you *always* until the end of the age," and Paul writes in Ephesians 3:20–21, "[T]o him be glory in the church and in Christ Jesus to *all generations, forever and ever.* Amen."

So which is more likely? Jesus Christ founded a Church in Israel that went out of existence after his Ascension, then founded another Church in America that also went out of existence a few centuries later, and then waited more than 1,000 years to restore his Church? Or the Church Jesus originally founded on Peter and the apostles never failed to exist, just as Jesus promised?

20. How should Catholics engage Mormon friends, family, and missionaries in dialogue?

Don't preach or accuse
Instead of launching into a full-frontal assault on the LDS faith, ask questions so that the other person can explain it to you. You can also use this opportunity to ask polite yet firm questions about Mormon teaching that are covered in this booklet. If you are engaging missionaries at your door, invite them inside and offer them water or juice (not alcohol, coffee, or tea!). This

gentle, questioning approach is more effective than giving a lecture.

Don't refer to the Mormon faith as a "cult"
The word *cult* has many different meanings, and it originally just meant a group of people who worship a God. Usually, a modern cult is dangerous in the sense that it isolates believers from friends and family and uses brainwashing or mind-control techniques in order to keep people from leaving. If you call Mormonism a cult, it will simply make you seem ignorant in the eyes of LDS people.

Don't refer to Mormonism as a "Christian" faith
As I've already shown, the Church of Jesus Christ of Latter-day Saints does not believe in the essential elements of the Christian faith. Calling the LDS faith "Christian" might prevent conflict, but it also prevents your Mormon friends from coming to know the true God of Christianity. When a Mormon asks you, "Why don't you think we're Christians?" You should respond, "I believe a Christian is anyone who worships the God of Christianity. Would you be willing to discuss with me who you believe the God of Christianity is to see if we worship the same God?"

One simple approach you can take is to say that you would join their church but you would miss praying to Jesus Christ, who is not your "eldest brother" but is, as the apostle Thomas said, your "Lord and God."

Do ask Mormons to defend the Great Apostasy
Tell your LDS friends that you agree with them that if Christ's Church fell into a total apostasy, then a restoration like theirs would be needed. You can even agree with them that Protestant Christianity is insufficient in its acceptance of *sola scriptura* and its denial of the need for a visible Church with a sacred hierarchy. But, if the Great Apostasy never took place, Christ's Church would still reign today, and that Church would be the Catholic Church.

You can press them further by asking, "Why should I believe that Jesus came to Earth to establish a Church, only to have it die right after he left, and then waited 1,800 years to reestablish it? What's wrong with believing that Jesus got it right the first time and the Church he founded still exists?"

The continual existence of Christ's Church also explains one of the key sources of Mormon doctrine—the Bible. If Mormons deny that the Catholic Church of the third and fourth centuries had apostolic authority, then they can't accept the Church's pronouncement of the canon of Scripture, the list of books that belong in the Bible. If they do accept the canon of Scripture, they should accept the authority of the Church that established the canon.[75]

Do give them your testimony
Testimonies are very important to the LDS faith, and Mormon missionaries will often share theirs with you

in lieu of a formal argument. In that case, it's perfectly acceptable for you to share your testimony about how the Catholic Church has helped you grow in your relationship with the person of Jesus Christ.

In your own testimony, you can emphasize what Catholics and Mormons share in common (rejection of *sola scriptura*, acceptance of a visible Church authority, rejection of salvation by faith alone, etc.) and also praise the unique elements of the Catholic Faith. This includes the intimate reality of Christ in the Eucharist, the healing power of the sacrament of reconciliation, the family found in the communion of saints, and the trustworthy foundation of a Church whose authority can be traced back to Jesus himself.

About the Author

Trent Horn is an apologist and speaker for Catholic Answers. He specializes in pro-life issues as well as outreach to atheists and agnostics. He holds a master's degree in theology from Franciscan University of Steubenville.

Endnotes

1 Doctrine and Covenants 1:30.

2 Available online at http://www.mormon.org/beliefs/joseph-smith.

3 Specifically, it accused Smith of introducing "a plurality of Gods above the God of this universe, and his liability to fall with all his creations; the plurality of wives, for time and eternity, the doctrine of unconditional sealing up to eternal life, against all crimes except that of sheding [sic] innocent blood." *Nauvoo Expositor.* Vol .1. No. 1. June 7, 1844.

4 While Smith said he was "going like a lamb to the slaughter" (Joseph Smith—History 1:17ff) and others have called him a "martyr," even LDS historians agree that Smith responded with violence against his killers. Smith was certainly murdered in cold blood, but he was only a "martyr" in the sense that he died because people disliked his religious beliefs, not because he voluntarily chose to die instead of renouncing his religious beliefs.

5 Available online at http://www.mormonnewsroom.org/article/15-million-member-milestone-announced-at-churchs-general-conference.

6 See Doctrine and Covenants 107:91–92.

7 Polygyny, which LDS are accused of practicing, is a form of polygamy that occurs when a man is married to more than one woman at a time. Polyandry occurs when a woman is married to more than one man at a time.

8 Todd Compton. *In Sacred Loneliness: The Plural Wives of Joseph Smith.* (Signature Books, 1997).

9 This is now referred to as "Declaration 1" and is available online

at https://www.lds.org/scriptures/dc-testament/od/1?lang=eng.

10 This is also called "Baptism for the Dead." To learn more about this subject, see the Catholic Answers tract, "Mormonism's Baptism for the Dead," available online at http://www.catholic.com/tracts/mormonisms-baptism-for-the-dead.

11 Available online at https://www.lds.org/topics/print/temples.

12 An official LDS blog states that "the Church revelation spelling out health practices does not mention the use of caffeine." Available online at http://www.mormonnewsroom.org/article/mormonism-news--getting-it-right-august-29.

13 *Gospel Principles*, Chapter 1.

14 St. Irenaeus, *Against Heresies* 2:13:3.

15 St. Thomas Aquinas, *Summa Contra Gentiles.* III.68.3.

16 See CCC 357.

17 Theologians call these appearances *theophanies*, and although they were examples of God appearing to human beings, they were not cases of human beings seeing God's true glory.

18 The interpretation of this verse in its literal sense is what Smith said in Doctrine and Covenants 130:3 was "old, sectarian, and false."

19 Joseph Smith Jr., "The King Follett Sermon," *Ensign*, May 1971, 13. Available online at https://www.lds.org/ensign/1971/04/the-king-follett-sermon?lang=eng.

20 William W. Phelps, "If you could hie to Kolob." Available online at https://www.lds.org/music/library/hymns/if-you-could-hie-to-kolob?lang=eng.

21 It's true that Genesis 1:26 uses the phrase "Let *us* make man in our image," but this does not imply the work of multiple Gods, as the single pronoun is still used in later verses. The words *us* and

our probably represent the "plural of majesty," or God speaking as more than one person because of how grand he is or because he is addressing his heavenly court. Isaiah 6:8 is an example of this: "Then I heard the voice of the Lord saying, "Whom shall I send, and who will go for us?" And I said, "Here am I; send me!"

22 A better term to use would be *henotheism*, or the worship of one God who is acknowledged to exist alongside many other Gods.

23 *Journal of Discourses* 17:143.

24 "Becoming like God." Available online at: https://www.lds.org/topics/becoming-like-god?lang=eng.

25 Matthew 5:44.

26 Ignatius. *Letter to the Magnesians,* 8:1.

27 See St. Thomas Aquinas, *Summa Theologica,* I.2.3.

28 See Trent Horn. *Answering Atheism: How to Make the Case for God with Logic and Charity* (Catholic Answers Press, San Diego, 2013) 123–136.

29 Lisa Grossman, "Why physicists can't avoid a creation event," *New Scientist Magazine,* 01/11/12.

30 Athanasius, *De Incarnatione,* I.

31 Jarolslav Pelikan, *Christianity and Classical Culture: The Metamorphosis of Natural Theology in the Christian Encounter with Hellenism* (Yale University Press, 1995), 318.

32 See CCC 292 and CCC 296.

33 *The Shepherd*, 1:1:1.

34 Eric Shuster, *Catholic Roots, Mormon Harvest* (Cedar Fort, Springville, 2009), 62.

35 This contradicts the Catholic view that "every spiritual soul is created immediately by God—it is not 'produced' by the parents"

(*Catechism of the Catholic Church*, 366).

36 "Origin of Man" Improvement Era, Nov. 1909, 75–81. Available
     online at https://www.lds.org/ensign/2002/02/the-origin-of-
     man?lang=eng.

37 See *Catechism of the Catholic Church*, 239.

38 "Origin of Man," 1909.

39 Brigham Young, *Journal of Discourses*, 8:115.

40 See http://en.fairmormon.org/Jesus_Christ/Brother_of_Satan.

41 *Catechism of the Catholic Church*, 464.

42 See *Catechism of the Catholic Church*, 444.

43 *Teachings of the Prophet Joseph Smith*, 372.

44 David Whitmer, "An Address to All Believers in Christ" (1887), 12.

45 Another piece of evidence against the Book of Mormon is
     that genetic evidence shows that Native Americans are the
     descendants of Asians who crossed a land bridge in Alaska, and
     not Semites from the Middle East.

46 Lucy Mack Smith, *Biographical Sketches of Joseph Smith The
     Prophet* (1902), Chapter 31.

47 *History of Joseph Smith, Jr.,* by himself, in Joseph Smith's Letter
     Book at Kirtland, November 27, 1832, to August 4, 1835 (Church
     Historian's Library, Salt Lake City, Utah).

48 See Eric Shuster and Charles Sale, *The Biblical Roots of
     Mormonism* (Cedar Fort, Springville, 2010), 83.

49 Marvin Hill, "Brodie Revisited: A Reappraisal" *Dialogue: A
     Journal of Mormon Thought* (Vol. 7, No. 4, 1972), 84–85.

50 Some critics allege that Sidney Rigdon or even Oliver Cowdery
     cowrote the book with Smith.

51 Lucy Mack Smith, *Biographical Sketches of Joseph Smith The*

Prophet (1902), 84.

52 Keep in the mind the same phrase is used less than five hundred times in the King James Bible, which is five times longer than the Book of Mormon. For response to arguments that "and it came to pass" is a faithful translation of the Hebrew word *Wayehi*, see Thomas Finley, "Does the Book of Mormon Reflect an Ancient Near Eastern Background?", *The New Mormon Challenge*, eds. Francis Beckwith, Carl Mosser, Paul Owen (Zondervan, Grand Rapids, 2002), 347–348.

53 Joseph Smith, *History* 1:53.

54 See B.H. Roberts, *Studies of the Book of Mormon*, (Signature Books, 1992).

55 CCC 66.

56 Correspondence from Julie Crain to Luke Wilson, August 12, 1998. Available online at: http://mit.irr.org/national-geographic-society-statement-on-book-of-mormon.

57 This has motivated some liberal LDS scholars to say that the Book of Mormon is not a literal history but an allegory meant to inspire faith.

58 Robert Bennett, *Leap of Faith: Confronting the Origins of the Book of Mormon* (Deseret Book Company, Salt Lake City, 2009), 189–191.

59 Rev. F.S. Spaulding, D.D., "Joseph Smith, Jr. As a Translator," Salt Lake City, Utah, November 1, 1912.

60 For example, Smith writes, "This after noon labored on the Egyptian alphabet, in company with bro. O. Cowdery and W. W. Phelps: the System of astronomy was unfolded." Diary of Joseph Smith, Thursday October 1, 1835.

61 See Deuteronomy 18:22 and Deuteronomy 13:18.

62 Canon 1141.

63 "The Family: A Proclamation to the World," The First Presidency and Council of the Twelve Apostles of the Church of Jesus Christ of Latter-Day Saints. Read by President Gordon B. Hinckley as part of his message at the General Relief Society Meeting held September 23, 1995, in Salt Lake City, Utah.

64 *Book 1 for Stake Presidents and Bishops*, Section 3.6.1, "Sealing of Living Members after a Spouse's Death" (2006), 85.

65 2 Nephi 22–23. Catholics agree with LDS that Adam's descendants are not "punished" for his particular sin. However, we do *share* in it because we inherited the corrupted, sinful nature Adam and Eve received through the fall (*Catechism of the Catholic Church*, 404) .

66 Romans 5:19.

67 *Gospel Principles*, Ch. 41. LDS usually defend this belief by appealing to 1 Peter 3:19, where it describes Christ preaching to the "spirits in prison." But this is a reference to the souls who died before the Resurrection. *Catechism of the Catholic Church* 633 says, "Jesus did not descend into hell to deliver the damned, nor to destroy the hell of damnation, but to free the just who had gone before him."

68 Doctrine and Covenants 76:89.

69 These "sons of perdition" are described in Doctrine and Covenants 76.

70 See 1 Nephi 13.

71 Clement, "Against Heresies," 1:462.

72 Ignatius, "To the Ephesians," 1:58.

73 See http://en.fairmormon.org/Apostasy/Not_complete.

74 Clement, *Letter to the Corinthians* 44:1–3.

75 For more information on this topic, see Devin Rose. *The Protestant's Dilemma: How the Reformation's Shocking Consequences Point to the Truth of Catholicism.* (Catholic Answers Press, San Diego, 2014).

Become part of the team.
Help support Catholic Answers.

Catholic Answers is an apostolate dedicated to serving Christ by bringing the fullness of Catholic truth to the world. We help good Catholics become better Catholics, bring former Catholics "home," and lead non-Catholics into the fullness of the Faith.

Catholic Answers neither asks for nor receives financial support from any diocese. The majority of its annual income is in the form of donations from individual supporters like you.

To make a donation by phone using your credit card, please speak with one of our customer service representatives at 888-291-8000.

To make a donation by check, please send a check payable to "Catholic Answers" to:

> Catholic Answers
> 2020 Gillespie Way
> El Cajon, CA 92020

To make a donation online, visit **catholic.com**.

catholic.com